the
POWER
of
COVERING

The Women's Reconnection to Her Spiritual Authority in Christ

Darlene M. Jackson

The Power of Covering

First Published 2024 by Darlene Jackson
www.tdcministry.com

Paperback ISBN: 979-8-9910826-1-7
Ebook ISBN: 979-8-9910826-0-0
Hardback ISBN: 979-8-9910826-2-4

Book Cover Design and Interior Formatting by 100Covers.

Table of Contents

Preface

"To The Ladies"

The covering of a woman's head is both physical and spiritual. A head covering is a physical object that serves a physical purpose, but when used for the spiritual purpose of prayer and prophesying, a woman's head covering becomes something else! In the realm of the Spirit it becomes a symbol of a husband's spiritual authority over the woman, that God and the angels recognize, which is *a benefit to the woman, not a burden!*

Consequently, if you don't know or understand how the things of the Spirit operate, then you cannot benefit from them. The reality is that many of God's children are ignorant of the workings of *His Spiritual Kingdom;* and it's because many are still trying to live on earth like mere men who are a part of *a religion;* instead of living like spiritual children and sons of God who belong to God's Kingdom.

By His grace, God's great love for us has provided a way for men & women to be covered under the *protective covering of His Word,* through a hierarchical order of His Kingdom. Therefore the idea of a woman "covering her head" according to her faith, does not come from the culture of the world, but it's an aspect of God's Kingdom!

We live according to "a Kingdom" not a religion

The *"born again"* experience is the Spiritual awakening of the **Spirit of man** *(our inner man)* being reborn of God's Spirit, into the consciousness and mind of Christ within God and His Kingdom.

> *"Children born not of blood, nor of the desire or will of man, but born of God." John 1:13 BSB*

> *"For you have been born again, not of perishable seed, but of imperishable, through the living and enduring word of God" 1 Peter 1:23*

It's the **Person of the Holy Spirit** *(the governor of God's Kingdom)* that teaches Christ's Church how to live on earth according to *the ways of God's Kingdom,* and not according to the *ways of a religion.*

Once *the soul* submits to following *the spirit*, the Holy Spirit reveals to our *inner spirit man,* the solution to our problem, **and our problem is how we think.** Our thoughts which come from the soul are in darkness; however according to the scriptures, this is the solution...

Romans 12 says,

> *"Do not be conformed to this world, but **be transformed by the renewing of your mind.** Then you will be able to test and approve what is the good, pleasing, and perfect will of God."*

Renew meaning- Take up again, come back to

The renewing of the mind is the process of the Holy Spirit, revealing the mind of Christ to us once again!

Let's look at this scripture again, but this time I want to share with you the way I heard the Lord speak it to me. I heard,

> *"Do not be conformed (**by your thinking**) to this world, but be transformed by (**allowing The Holy Spirit**) the renewing of your mind (**revealing to you the mind of Christ**). Then you will be able to discern (**according to His perspective**) what is the good, pleasing, and perfect will of God." Romans 12:2 BSB*

Philippians 2:5 says,

> *"**Let this mind** be in you which was also in Christ Jesus," NKJV*

Everyday, our relationship with God by His Spirit, should be leading us to demonstrate outward aspects of God's Kingdom, through the **mind of Christ!**

This means we must learn to follow the *spiritual laws and culture of Christ's Kingdom,* which includes the *laws of covering. Spiritual covering* functions according to a hierarchical order that requires our submission. God has assigned a specific *order of covering* over man, because every level of *covering* functions according to a purpose.

Hence, the *culture of the world* didn't create the idea for a woman *to cover her head.* The *"Covering"* that comes out of the world is an imitation, a perverted version of a reality that comes out of God's Kingdom!

Therefore, the inspired writings in this book given to me by the Holy Spirit, teaches women *who are born again of God's Spirit* how to live in the world according to the *mind of Christ* and the *culture of God's Kingdom;* through the Spirit's expression of **submission to God's order of authority.**

For all women in Christ have access (*by proximity*) to authority, but all don't have *"possession to exercise"* authority until they FIRST exercise **submission to authority!**

Introduction

The Worlds Covering

Let me start by making this statement, *"I've come to understand that **head covering** for women is **a truth** that has to be revealed, just like truth the Spirit of God reveals in other areas of our lives concerning His Kingdom."* One thing is sure, once truth is revealed, it has to be received in order for that truth to produce in you! Within the body of Christ, many men and women are knowingly and some unknowingly rejecting truth concerning the spiritual aspect of *a woman covering her head,* and it's because of a connection to the *culture of the world.*

How do I know? Because I was connected to *the culture of the world*! This book is the revealed knowledge of the *truth of covering* that was shown to me, and commanded for me to write, by the Spirit of God.

The first thing the Spirit of God revealed to me, was the influence of the world's culture I was under and I didn't know it! I was under the world's influence because I followed the opinions of the culture concerning its standard of beauty concerning how I should look. **Covering my head was not something I considered.** What I considered was the world's ways and the cultures standards, *I did not consider God's ways and His standards!*

Most of the arguments today about women covering their head comes from the same worldly perspective which only considers why women DON'T *have to cover their head;* most don't consider (***God's perspective***) *why women should cover their head!* As Children of God, there are always benefits that come when we choose to live according to God's Kingdom. Spiritual benefits are restored to *women in Christ,* who choose to cover their head!

So over the next few chapters, I'm going to discuss what the Lord showed me concerning *what spiritual Covering is, the influence of the worlds culture upon women of the Church, the physical & spiritual purpose for our head & hair, what spiritual authority is and how to exercise authority, the difference between anointing and authority, the spiritual perspective of covering from the beginning, why & when should a women cover her head, and the spiritual benefit to a woman who covers her head.*

However, before I can talk to you about *"why women should cover their head,"* the Lord wants to expose the root behind why so many women within the body of Christ **don't cover their head,** considering this is where the Lord started with me. He didn't just say one day, *"Darlene I want you to cover your head,"* no! God first had to open my eyes to the spiritual root of darkness (*from the world's culture*) that was in me, that I was unknowingly connected to!

The following pages tell how God revealed the truth to me concerning *the darkness of the culture,* and *God's purpose for covering* that comes out of the laws of God's Kingdom.

Chapter 1

Exposing the dark root of the influence of Culture

It started in July of 2022, I was making plans to go on vacation to celebrate my 50th birthday in September, and for the first time, I struggled with the idea of putting braiding hair extensions in my hair. I mean I really, really, wrestled with thoughts of *"get the braiding extensions, it will make your vacation easier,"* against thoughts of *"no don't get the braids, save the money."* However every time I leaned towards not getting braids, the question, *"but what are you going to do with your hair everyday"* would come to my mind. So now what seemed to be a "no brainer" decision for me in the past, has now become a full on struggle for me to pull the trigger to do.

Then around mid-August (*with still no decision made about getting braids*) as I'm watching YouTube videos, I came across a thumbnail picture of a young Black woman with **long braids, long eye lashes, and long nails,** and I immediately hear the Holy Spirit say,

"That's a look!"

Now when I heard this statement I had no idea what God meant, or where He was going with this statement, but He continued on and said to me,

> *"That look is **an identifying marker** for the children of darkness, identifying that their heart and mind belong **to the Spirit of this world.**"*

In other words, the Holy Spirit was saying that a person's *inward heart & mindset,* produces an *outward look!*

Let me say that again,

> *"Our **inward mindset**
> produces an **outward look!**"*

So whatever we believe and have received in our heart and soul, it manifests physically, in *what we say, in what we do, and **in how we look!***

> NOTE:[Please understand, I did **NOT** receive a word concerning wearing fake eyelashes and fake nails, so I'm not saying wearing those things are wrong or right; I'm only highlighting and sharing what the Lord revealed and spoke to me at that moment.]

The Lord showed me that just like that young woman in the thumb-nail picture, I too had **believed** and **received** a spiritual influence from the world that was producing that same *"look of the world"* in me. I was trying to maintain an outward standard of beauty according to the *standards of the world*, and not according to the standard of God! Woo! Jesus! That needs repeating...

> *"I saw myself outwardly according to the standards of the world, and NOT according to* **the standard of God!"**

I was more concerned with how the world and other people saw me, than I was with how God saw me. The **world's standard** focuses on the outer man, it's all about how someone looks on the outside; and it was at this moment of spiritual awakening, the Lord reminded me *"the source of my beauty is* **inward** *not outward!"*

The Scripture says,

> *"Do not love the world or anything in the world. If any-one loves the world, the love of the Father is not in him. For all that is in the world—the desires of the flesh, the desires of the eyes, and the pride of life—is not from the* **Father but from the world."** *1 John 2:15-16 ESV*

The culture of the world is built on three things, **the desires of the flesh, the desires of the eyes, and the pride of life**, because the purpose of culture is to influence! The purpose of the world's culture is to influence us to partake of it! The culture of the world is taught by demons through *"the doctrine of demons."* The word "doctrine" simply means "to teach." Demons *teach* a *culture of darkness* that influences a lifestyle around, the desires of the flesh, the desires of the eyes, and the pride of life. Reality television shows like Love and Hip Hop, House Wives and Basketball Wives, are all examples of a "culture of darkness" taught by demonic influences, through the system of media, influencing a lifestyle of the flesh, the desires of the eyes, and the pride of life. How we live, what we eat, our music, the way we think (*our ideology and beliefs*) and our appearance are all influenced by the culture of the world through the doctrine of demons.

So if watching those reality tv shows bother you, or you find yourself turning away from them, and not watching them, it's not just because you think they portray women or the Black community in a negative way, it's because you're responding to the Holy Spirits guidance, leading you away from a spiritual influence that's not His!

APPEARANCE -VS- A LOOK

God said to me,

> *"The culture of the world produces a look the culture of God's Kingdom produces **an appearance**!*
>
> *A Look - describes physical qualities that can be seen.*
>
> *Appearance means; the act of appearing **or coming into sight**; the act of becoming visible to the eye.*

Now here's the question, "what is becoming visible in us (*believers in Christ*) to others? Answer, **the image of Christ!** We should be revealing Christ everyday to the world!

Our appearance as Believers should be bringing what is *unseen* into what can be *seen*, for the purpose of affecting our environment. God is not into making *something look good*, just for the sake of *looking good.* God is in the business of revealing **the substance of His Kingdom through us.**

The Lord took me to Luke 8:27 to illustrate this understanding....

*"When Jesus stepped ashore, He was met by a demon-possessed man from the town. For a long time this man had not worn clothing or lived in a house, but he stayed in the tombs. When the man saw Jesus, he cried out and fell down before Him, shouting in a loud voice, "What do You want with me, Jesus, Son of the Most High God? I beg You not to torture me!" For Jesus had commanded the unclean spirit to come out of the man. Many times it had seized him, and though he was bound with chains and shackles, he had broken the chains and been driven by the demon into solitary places. "What is your name?" Jesus asked. "Legion," he replied, because many demons had gone into him. And the demons kept begging Jesus not to order them to go into the Abyss. There on the hillside a large herd of pigs was feeding. So the demons begged Jesus to let them enter the pigs, and He gave them permission. Then the demons came out of the man and went into the pigs, and the herd rushed down the steep bank into the lake and was drowned. When those tending the pigs saw what had happened, they ran off and reported this in the town and countryside. So the people went out to see what had happened. They came to Jesus and found the man whom **the demons had left, sitting at Jesus' feet, clothed and in his right mind;** and they were afraid." ESV*

The Spirit of God said to me,

> *"When the people came to Jesus and found the man from whom the demons had gone out, **what was his appearance?**"*

- *he was **sitting down** (at the feet of Jesus),*
- *he was **clothed,** and*
- *in his **right mind,***

The man now had *an appearance* indicating his encounter with Jesus produced an inward change! The man no longer had an *outward physical look* indicating he belonged to the darkness. The change that occurred on the *inside* of the man, was now reflected in his appearance to the people on the outside *(he was sitting down, clothed and in his right mind)*.

The man's outward appearance was reflective of the inward power of the Kingdom of Christ!

> *"Christ and His Kingdom on the inside of us, is the substance that produces an outward appearance of an inward change to others, in those who are yielded to His Spirit!"*

Now, please hear me, I don't believe God is saying that we should not care about how we look physically. There's nothing wrong with wanting to style your hair or your body fashionably according to your style and personality; however we must remember, that our *Life in Christ* is not about beautifying the outward body, but it's about allowing the life of Christ to beautify our soul, and allow that inward beauty to manifest outward to effect and transform the lives of others!

Chapter 2

There's A Physical Representation With A Spiritual Purpose for Everything!

Did you know that our **HEAD** and the **HAIR** on our head are physical representations that reveal a spiritual purpose in the realm of the Spirit?

*"And even the very **hairs of your head** are all numbered."*
Luke 12:7

Physical Representations

Physical representations - are signs, symbols, likeness or image of something that speaks to God's purposes.

One day I heard the Lord say,

> *"The physical body of man was prepared for the day of man's disobedience! God knows all things, and all possibilities, therefore everything concerning man from his beginning was planned, even the consequences for his choice, was built into creation from the beginning! No matter the choice, God ensured that man would have the capacity and the ability to fulfill God's purpose, whether man chose life or death! God prepared in advance how the body of man would function and live in a consciousness of disobedience and darkness!"*

Hebrews 10:5 says,

> *"Consequently, when Christ came into the world, he said, "Sacrifices and offerings you have not desired, but a body have you prepared for me." ESV*

The Lord said to me,

> *"Man's body was prepared for the consequence of darkness! For in the day that man falls, Christ's spiritual authority that he carries on the inside of his body, is represented on the outside of his body."*

But why does the outside of man's body need to carry representations of Christ's authority? Who are these outward representations on display for? Ephesians 3:10 tells us,

> *"So that the manifold wisdom of God might now be made known through the church to the rulers and the authorities in the heavenly places." NASB 1995*

The outward body (*like the hair on our head*) carries physical representations of Christ's spiritual authority. However, when man dwelled in the spiritual consciousness of Christ in the garden, the physical properties of hair on man's head was **not** needed, meaning hair did not need to be seen as a symbol of Christ's authority.

It was only after the fall of man, that hair began to be used for man's *physical existence, his consciousness on the earth*; while at the same time it reveals the symbol of Christ's authority to the spiritual rulers and authorities in the heavenly places.

Spiritual Purpose for the "HEAD & HAIR"

Everything in the physical earth that can be seen with the eyes has a physical purpose; but in the unseen realm, there is a spiritual counterpart that reveals a spiritual purpose too.

For example, Olive oil in the natural realm serves a physical purpose as a *cooking oil*, but it's also used within the Church as an *anointing oil*, serving a different function and purpose in the realm of the Spirit.

So even though we know that the hair on our head serves a physical purpose, hair is a representation, a symbol for something spiritually unseen, that's occurring in the realm of the Spirit.

> *"The Holy Spirit showed me **the hair on our head represents the covering authority of Christ!** Hair is the outward physical symbol for Christ's spiritual authority over man on the earth."*

This is why many people who wear their hair long (like locs) say they feel like their hair holds power like Samson, or they believe their hair is spiritual. Well to that point they're right! It's not because of the hair style though, it's because of what hair represents!

> *"Hair represents Christ's power and authority that covers man!"*

Then the Lord went further and He showed me that the physical head of man also has Spiritual representations!

The physical head represents ***the spiritual mind.*** I'll say that again,

> *The physical **HEAD** represents the Spiritual **MIND**.*

Here's an example, Colossians 1:18 ESV says,

> ***"Christ is the HEAD of the Church,"***

In other words, Christ is the ***mind*** (*the head*) of the ***body*** (*the church*); and the mind (*the head*) governs the body (*the church*).

So in this physical realm we have a *head*, but in the realm of the spirit the counterpart to *the head* is the operation of *a mind!*

- The **head** = The **mind**
          &
- **Hair** = Christ's **authority**

In the natural realm, hair is a physical protective covering over our physical head; but in the spiritual realm, spiritual beings (*of light and darkness*) don't see hair, they see spiritual authority! In other words, to Spirits the "physical strands of hair" on the head of man, is seen as a symbol ***of Christ's spiritual authority, a crown upon man's head!***

This is what I heard,

> *"Mankind wears on his head a **crown**, symbolizing Christ's spiritual authority, which is man's cover."*

This is why the highest point on the top of our head where our hair grows is called

> ***"the crown of the head."***

Job 2:7 says,

> *"So Satan went out from the presence of the* LORD, *and struck Job with painful boils from the sole of his foot to the crown of his head."* ESV

What is a crown?

> ***A Crown is circular;*** *it's the top or highest part; a royal or imperial headdress of sovereignty.*

Well the hair on our head grows from the "crown point" of the scalp and grows in a *circular* formation. A coincidence? Not at all.

In the old testament scriptures, a Nazarite's dedication of worship to God was through the uncut physical hair on the head.

Numbers 6:7 says,

> ***"The crown of consecration to God is upon his head."***
> *ESV*

Proverbs 16:31 says,

> *"Gray hair is a crown of glory; it is attained along the path of righteousness."ESV*

Job 19:10 says,

> *"He has stripped me of my glory, And taken the crown from my head." ESV*

When Job said, *"he was stripped of his glory,"* he was referring to losing his gray hair because of his affliction; *his gray hair was the crown of glory* that was taken from his head.

> NOTE: [*All men born on the earth have been given the natural propensity to grow hair (the symbol of Christ's authority) on their head. The failure to grow hair, or to retain hair is a physical consequence of the spiritual death that came upon man through Adam's rebellion; that opened the door to Satan's ability to attack man's symbol of authority through sicknesses, disease and stress, things that cause hair loss, or prevent hair growth.*]

So here's the question I heard :

> *"If the natural hair on our head has a spiritual representation and purpose, then what is the spiritual purpose behind hair weaves, wigs and extensions? What do they represent in the realm of the spirit?"*

Good question, let's explore their purpose further!

Chapter 3

The Deceptive Purpose of Hair Extensions & Wigs

*NOTE: [This chapter is not about attacking women who choose to wear wigs, weaves, or extensions; it's about revealing the deceptive ways the enemy brings God's people into **agreement with the darkness of the world!** As a result, many of us within the Church are deeply rooted in the ways of the world and we don't even know it!]*

Let me reiterate once again, that there's a Spirit behind everything! Behind every thought, every idea, name, invention, philosophy, behind every law, language, religion, belief, tradition, culture, action and word that manifests in the earth! Whether these spirits are of light or darkness, both are purposed to influence mankind in order to bring forth the plans and purpose of *a Kingdom* into the earth!

So with this understanding on the forefront of your mind, let's examine the names given to *"hair extensions"*

- Synthetic hair *(because it's made of chemicals)*
- Imitation hair
- Fake hair
- Artificial hair
- Human hair
- Temple hair *(hair cut from a woman's head for the purpose of a sacrifice to an Idol God or Deity.)*

With the exception of human hair and temple hair, from the list, these names tell us what wigs and hair extensions are, they are **counterfeit recreations** for the natural hair that God created! I mean back in the day we used to say stuff like "why is she wearing that "fake hair." Well another word for fake is counterfeit.

> **Counterfeit** means to imitate something authentic, with the intent to deceive, steal, destroy, or replace the original….

And who is the great deceiver, imitator and **counterfeiter** of the world? **Satan!** Satan's Kingdom is the influence behind the billion dollar beauty industry system, that convinces the world that beauty is skin deep, according to what we see on the outside.

The Scripture says of Lucifer (who is Satan),

> 'You were the seal of perfection, full of wisdom **and perfect in beauty…**

Wait, **perfect in beauty?** Isn't that Satan's influence over the world today? Men and especially women, are seeking ways to be perfect in beauty! Hair extensions, wigs, hair implants, cosmetic procedures such as BBL's (*Brazilian butt lift*), tummy tucks, breast implants, fake nails, excessive makeup, and hair coloring, are all ways of trying to achieve a level of perfection in outward beauty!

Ezekiel 28:17 says of Satan,

> *"Your heart grew proud of your beauty; you corrupted your wisdom because of your splendor;" ESV*

Therefore, because Satan corrupted his wisdom, it's this same corrupted wisdom that has perverted how men and women see beauty, which most tend to see beauty as something outward according to the flesh. Most people don't see beauty as something inward, according to our Spirit.

> *"I was trying to maintain an outward standard of beauty that I saw as physically pleasing to the eye."*

An Insufficient Covering

As the Spirit of the Lord opened my eyes to see the truth that the source of my beauty lies within, the Lord showed me whenever I wore a wig, I was using one of Satan's *counterfeit coverings to cover my* hair!

Corinthians 11:15 ESV says,

> *"Long hair is given to her (the women) as a covering."*

In other words by choosing to wear another covering **over my covering** *(my hair)* that did not come from God, I was coming under an insufficient covering.

God asked me a question, He said,

"Why are wigs an insufficient way for women to cover their head?"

The answer, because *the Spiritual intent behind wigs* weren't purposed to cover! Wigs are a perversion because they were purposed to **replace,** and **to mimic** natural hair that grows from the head, to replace the purpose God gave us of our natural hair as a covering.

However, hats and scarves are purposed to *cover the head* as a secondary physical covering to keep in the source of heat generated from the body that escapes through the top of the head. Wigs and weaves however were not purposed to maintain body warmth, (even though you can use them in that way), the spirit behind their use is to pervert God's intentions for our natural hair to be a covering.

Many of us Christian women, out of our ignorance to God's spiritual ways, are unknowingly rejecting God's *provision of covering*, and we're choosing a counterfeit covering when we cover our head with *processed or artificial hair.* Let's be honest ladies, when it comes to the culture (especially within the black community), most of us have adopted and normalized mixing with the culture of the world, which keeps the spiritual authority of the women subdued through what I heard the Lord call *Spiritual Mixing.*

Spiritual Mixing

"A little leaven works through the whole batch of dough."
Galatians 5:9 BSB

This is the definition I received from the Lord,

> *Spiritual Mixing - Two seeds from separate sources; spiritual agreement between the seed of light and the seed of darkness.*

The Lord said, *"This is what took place in the garden of Eden between Eve and the Serpent."* The woman received the word of the Serpent, meaning she received his seed;

Genesis 3:14-16 ESV

> *"So the Lord God said to the serpent: Because you have done this, You are cursed more than all cattle, And more than every beast of the field; On your belly you shall go, And you shall eat dust All the days of your life. **And I will put enmity Between you and the woman, And between your seed and her Seed;** He shall bruise your head, And you shall bruise His heel."*

Eve was a carrier of the *seed of light*, **and** the serpent's *seed of darkness!* In the natural realm when a woman receives and carries two separate seeds from separate acts of sexual intercourse, it's called **Superfecundation**; the conceiving of twins with different fathers.

However from the beginning, God never intended for light and darkness to mix. In fact, the first thing God did after He spoke, *"let there Be light and saw that the light was good,"* was separate the light from the darkness. Genesis 1:3-4

Leviticus 19:19 ESV says,

> *"You shall not crossbreed **two different kinds of livestock**;
> You shall not sow your fields with **two kinds of seed**;
> and you shall not wear clothing made of **two kinds of
> material**."*

In other words the Lord is saying through these scriptures

> *"**Do not mix two different seeds!**"*

Both kingdoms; God's Kingdom of light and Satan's Kingdom of darkness need our agreement (*which takes place when we receive a seed from a spirit in our heart*), in order to operate and be effective in our lives. Now when it comes to following the world's standard of beauty, many of us Christian women have unknowingly come into agreement with the standard of the world, which means we have *Spiritual mixing* occurring within our heart. Another way to see this spiritual mixing of light with darkness according to the scriptures is called *spiritual agreement.*

2 Corinthians 14-17 says,

> *"What fellowship does light have with darkness? What harmony is there between Christ and Belial? Or what does a believer have in common with an unbeliever What agreement can exist between the temple of God and idols? For we are the temple of the living God. As God has said:*

> *"I will dwell with them and walk among them, and I will be their God, and they will be My people."*

"Therefore come out from among them and be separate, says the Lord." ESV

Here's a practical example of how ***spiritual mixing*** operates;

When a woman gets hair extensions (human or synthetic), braided in, sewn in, glued in or bonded; the hair extension is *blended together with the natural hair* on a woman's head. This physical blending together represents ***spiritual agreement***.

I heard the Lord say,

> *"Hair extensions blended together with the natural hair is an outward physical picture representing spiritual agreement, a compromise, a mixing with darkness that's taking place within the heart!"*

The word ***compromise*** means to weaken; so when we spiritually mix the light of Christ in our heart with darkness, this weakens our use and purpose by God, and allows Satan the advantage of bringing forth his corrupted purpose.

When I talk about how compromise weakens us, the scriptures about Samson and Delilah come to my mind. Samson compromised his strength (his hair), which left him weakened by its effects (the cutting of his hair). The compromise came because Samson did not ***reject the darkness!*** He did not turn away from the Spirit of darkness that influenced Delilah to get Samson to divulge his secret behind his strength in order to subdue him and destroy him! Instead Samson continued to play in Delilah's game of darkness, and he allowed himself to be entertained by the darkness, he cohabitated with the darkness, until he succumbed to the ways of darkness and told Delilah the secret to his strength;

*"And it came about, when she pressed him daily with her words and urged him, that his soul was annoyed to death. **So he told her all that was in his heart** and said to her, "A razor has never come on my head, for I have been a Nazirite to God from my mother's womb. If I am shaved, then my strength will leave me and I will become weak and be like any other man." Judges 16:15-17 ESV*

God said to me,

"When you have given your heart to something, you can easily be persuaded and manipulated."

Proverbs 4:23 says,

"Keep your heart with all vigilance, for from it flow the springs of life."ESV

Spiritual mixing is a picture that reveals our entertainment with darkness! Therefore when we belong to God, yet we're entertaining and cohabiting with darkness through the culture of the world, then we are as a harlot to God!

Think about it, what was Israel's constant sin before God? It was their **spiritual mixing** with the beliefs, customs and cultures of other nations! Israel gave themselves over to the culture and customs of neighboring nations around them, by mixing their belief and worship of God (Yahweh) with worship and sacrifice to other Gods and idols, which represented spiritual *prostitution* and *harlotry* to God. The Lord God showed me the difference between the two...

Israel's "prostitution" was their physical acts of intimacy through rituals, and worship ceremonies involving the building of altars, idols and sacrifices to their false Gods; in exchange for fertility, prosperity, and protection from these false Gods.

*"A **harlot**, the Lord said, enjoys from her heart giving herself over to someone; harlotry is an inward enjoyment that comes out of your heart!"*

Well the Lord showed me I was a harlot! I was a harlot because I belonged to God, yet I ***was enjoying from my heart assimilating with another Spirit***, I was enjoying receiving another spirit's seed! That's because I was under another spiritual covering and I did not know it!

As a wife, and mother of 2, wearing wigs brought the comfort and ease of a quick, easy yet fashionable lifestyle. God however, is not interested in making me comfortable with things that are quick, easy or fashionable from the world. He's interested in training my soul in righteousness, having intimacy and fellowship with me, and exercising my Spirit's authority in Christ over the territories *(my community, city and nation)* of the earth. God's will is for us to be separate from the darkness of the world, not to compromise and mix with it!

"Therefore come out from among them and be separate, says the Lord." 2 Corinthians ESV

As children of God, we can't say we belong to God on the inside, and look like the children of the world on the outside. Who you belong to on the inside *(in your heart and mind)*, that same ownership should be reflected on the outside!

The Lord said to me,

> *"The culture of Braids and wigs acts as **a decoy** to lure and entice us (women) to partake, to come into agreement with the purpose of darkness, with words like*

> ***"protective hair style", and "give your natural hair a break"***

> *But the decoy is not for those who belong to the darkness, the decoy is for those who are **of the light**, to draw us away from God's intended purpose, and back into mixing with the things of darkness, which makes the authority of Christ in us (women) little, to no effect!"*

That's Satan's purpose, to keep the seed of the woman mixing with the things of darkness, and disconnected from the authority of Christ! And Satan does it through deceiving the women to remain subject to the chaos *(disorder)* of the world, instead of the women being subject to the spirit, and the order *(the covering)* of God's Kingdom!"

Chapter 4

Satan's Chaos -VS- God's Order

I heard the Holy Spirit say,

> *"Through head covering we (women) are learning how to walk according to the order of God's Kingdom and not according to Satan's chaos (disorder) of the world."*

Satan is not all knowing, he just knows how God's Kingdom operates because he used to be a part of it! Therefore Satan knows the spiritual realms of God operate according to an *order of authority,* and authority flows through being subject to authority. Satan also knows the way to be disconnected from exercising authority, which is through rebellion to authority! This is what caused Satan to be disconnected from his authority as *"the anointed cherub who covers."*

"You were anointed as a guardian cherub, for I had ordained you. You were on the holy mountain of God; you walked among the fiery stones. From the day you were created you were blameless in your ways—until wickedness was found in you." Ezekiel 28:14 ESV

~ Satan's Chaos ~

Satan caused chaos *(disorder)* between the man *(the spirit)* and the woman *(the soul)* in order to disconnect them **both** from their God given authority and dominion over the earth. And how did Satan get them to disconnect from their authority? Through deception! The Serpent deceived the woman to rebel against the command of God which was given to her through *(the man)* her husband.

Genesis 2:15-17 ESV

"The LORD God took the man and put him in the garden of Eden to work it and keep it. And the LORD God commanded the man, saying, "You may surely eat of every tree of the garden, but of the tree of the knowledge of good and evil you shall not eat, for in the day that you eat of it you shall surely die."

Genesis 3 ESV

"Now the serpent was more crafty than any other beast of the field that the LORD God had made. He said to the woman, "Did God actually say, 'You shall not eat of any tree in the garden'?" And the woman said to the serpent, "We may eat of the fruit of the trees in the garden, but God said, "You shall not eat of the fruit of the tree that is in the midst of the garden, neither shall you touch it, lest you die."

NOTE: [The Lord showed me in verse 3 when Eve says "or touch it," it is an exaggeration. The Lord asked me "but why was Eve's statement to the Serpent exaggerated?" The Lord said, "because it was second hand information!" The command was given to the man, and the man gave the instruction to the women. This is what can happen to information that is 'passed on.'"]

According to God's order of creation, God commanded the man not to eat from the tree; then God made the woman from man's rib, and brought her to the man. Therefore what the woman knew concerning God's command, came through the voice of her husband. The woman however, made the choice to listen *to the word of the Serpent* instead of God's command through the voice of her husband, and the man heeded the voice of the women, instead of the voice of God..

But the serpent said to the woman, "You will not surely die. For God knows that when you eat of it your eyes will be opened, and you will be like God, knowing good and evil." So when the woman saw that the tree was good for food, and that it was a delight to the eyes, and that the tree was to be desired to make one wise, she took of its fruit and ate, and she also gave some to her husband who was with her, and he ate." Genesis 3:4-7 ESV

Through this deception, Satan caused (chaos) *disorder to God's order of authority!* Therefore, man's soul and spirit were no longer in union with God's Spirit, causing the spirit of man to go dormant, and the soul of man (*the woman, now out of God's alignment*) to no longer desire to follow after the Spirit, but now the soul follows the desire of the flesh to be the one in authority.

Genesis 3 ESV says,

> *"Your desire will be for your husband's (authority),*
> *Yet he will rule over you (by authority)."*

Hence the fall of man and the beginning of a perverted world of chaos and disorder! The world that God had created was changed, but the Word of God that established God's order of authority, *has never changed!*

> *"God's original idea for mankind to subdue and have dominion over the earth, through submission to the order and authority of Christ has never changed!"*

When Paul told the Church of Corinth that women should cover their heads *(when they pray or prophesy)* he was teaching the Church the ways of God's Kingdom. He was encouraging them to keep the traditions they learned from him, about *Christ's Kingdom* that are still the same! That's what Paul meant when he said *"follow me as I follow Christ," (as he follows the ways of Christ's Kingdom).*

We have to allow the Holy Spirit to change our thinking from we're a part of a religion, to seeing ourselves as a part of God's government kingdom. Within this Kingdom there is a culture (*like any earthly kingdom*), there are laws and an order of authority that we must be willing to learn and to follow!

"God said, let them have dominion over the Earth,"

As children of God and citizens of God's Kingdom, we have to understand the bigger picture of what Satan is after. Satan wants to weaken Christ's authority in man, because it's Christ's authority activated in man that subdues Satan's Kingdom of darkness!

"Satan doesn't create anything but He PERVERTS everything!"

In other words, in this physical realm of the Earth, any spiritual influence that is from Satan that influences man to create, may look like a *"new creation,"* but it is not a new creation but an *"old perversion"* from what God has already created!

Ecclesiastes 1:9 says,

"History merely repeats itself. It has all been done before. Nothing under the sun is truly new. ESV

When we as women of Christ's Kingdom don't seek the Spirit of God to determine the spirit behind *"why"* we desire to wear hair wigs, or *"why"* we desire to wear our natural hair mixed with hair weave, we may find ourselves subjected under another covering which is of darkness. That darkness has a purpose to weaken and hinder our spiritual authority and dominion in Christ!

Yes ladies, I know you may have your own purpose *"for why"* you wear wigs and weaves that can range from wanting to cover the effects of thinning hair or baldness due to cancers, illness or diseases, to using wigs and weaves in order to stay relevant with the culture, to masking underlying issues of low self esteem. Whatever "your why" or your purpose is, it **does not override Satan's purpose** for influencing you to wear them in the first place!

James 1:13 says,

*"When tempted, no one should say, "God is tempting me." For God cannot be tempted by evil, nor does He tempt anyone. But each one is tempted when **by his own evil desires** he is lured away and enticed. Then after*

desire has conceived, it gives birth to sin; and sin, when it is full-grown, gives birth to death." ESV

Have you ever considered that your desire to wear wigs and weaves is influenced by a Spirit that has an evil purpose that doesn't align with God's purpose for you? Now please hear me when I say this,

> *"I am not eliminating the possibility that in God's sovereignty, He can certainly influence someone to create wigs & hair extensions and/or wear them! However this would be on the basis of His Spirit's intent (**which is always good**), to fulfill His purpose, not your purpose or the world's purpose; because what makes knowledge good or evil is the intent and its purpose!*

So what we as Believers should learn to always seek, is understanding. We should first seek the Spirit of God to understand, *"what spirit is behind my desire to wear wigs, weaves and hair extensions,* is that spirit from God? When we understand the purpose or the spirit of a thing, truth is illuminated *so you see your desire correctly,* through the eyes of God's Spirit and not through the eyes of your flesh! Once we see our desire correctly, the choices we make will align with life and not death!

~ *God's Order* ~

The Lord began to show me God's order of authority *(which is His covering over man),* exists in the realm of the spirit. However, God's order was also represented in the *physical covering* over the tabernacle.

The tabernacle in Israel was the sanctuary of God, a physical dwell-ing place that was symbolic of the body of man, the place where God would once again dwell; and that physical tabernacle had *a covering*. God gave Moses detailed instructions on how to lay the physical coverings over the tabernacle. The coverings consisted of 4 layers made of different materials; **linen, goats hair, rams skins and badger skins.** Notice in the picture below, *the position of the coverings, how they OVERLAP one another.* Exodus 26 describes these 4 layers...

1. **Badger skins** - (Exodus 26:14) *Represents GOD*

2. **Rams skins** - dyed red (Exodus 26:14) *Represents CHRIST*

"You shall also make a covering of ram skins dyed red for the tent, and a covering of badger skins above that."

3. **Goats hair** (Exodus 26:7) *Represents MAN*

"You are to make curtains of goat hair for the tent over the tabernacle —eleven curtains in all."

4. Fine linen (Exodus 26:1-14) *Represents* WOMAN

*"You are to construct the tabernacle itself with ten curtains of **finely spun linen**, each with blue, purple, and scarlet yarn, and cherubim skillfully worked into them."*

Now notice the order that Paul spoke about in 1 Corinthians 11:3,

"But I want you to understand that
the head of every man is Christ,
and the head of the woman is man,
and the head of Christ, is God."

This order is not coincidental! The overlapping & layering of the material over the top of the tabernacle represents God *over Christ*, Christ *over man*, and man *over woman*. The tabernacle was symbolic of the body of man; and its physical coverings over the tabernacle, was symbolic of God's Spiritual *covering of authority over man*.

Chapter 5

Who Should Cover Their Head?

> *"But I want you to understand that the head of every man is Christ and the head of the woman is man, and the head of Christ is God. Every man who prays or prophesies with his head covered dishonors his head. And every woman who prays or prophesies with her head uncovered dishonors her head, for it is just as if her head were shaved." 1 Corinthians 11:3-5 ESV*

The Head of "EVERY man" is Christ

The definition of *"every"* in verse 3 of 1 Corinthians 11 refers broadly to *all the members of a group*. This means *"every man"* refers to all the members of *mankind,* which consists of man & woman. So the verse *"the head of every man is Christ,"* speaks to Christ as the head *over all,* over man & woman.

However, Paul does **not** say *"the head of every woman is man,"* the scripture says,

"The head of the woman *is man* (*is her husband*). That's because man is not the authority or the head over EVERY woman!

1 Corinthians 7:2 says it this way,

> *"But because of the temptation to sexual immorality,* ***each man should have his own wife and each woman her own husband." ESV***

In other words, each man should have authority over his own wife. Therefore Paul is making a distinction between *the head* of the woman, which is man (her husband), from the head of *every man & woman* which is Christ! This is God's order of authority over mankind, which starts with Christ;

Paul says,

- *But I want you to understand that **the head** of every man **is Christ***
- *and **the head of the woman is man***
- *and **the head of Christ is God***

Now there is another reference to *every,* in verses 4 & 5 that says *"every man"* and *"every woman."* However this meaning of *every,* speaks specifically to the ***individual group*** of man and the ***individual group*** of woman;

> *"**Every man** who prays or prophesies with his head covered dishonors his head And **every woman** who prays or prophesies with her head uncovered dishonors her head." 1 Corinthians 11:4-5 ESV*

For mankind, *hair* is the outward symbol of man's spiritual authority in Christ. This is why Paul says,

> *Every man who prays or prophesies with his head covered dishonors **his head**;" (meaning he dishonors Christ).*
> *1 Corinthians 11:4*

> *"For a man should not have his head covered, (when he prays or prophesies) since **he is the image and glory of God**,"*
> *1 Corinthians 11:7*

Therefore when a man prays or prophesies, he should **not** cover his head because he reveals the image and glory of God.

However, when it comes to the woman, here's what the Holy Spirit revealed to me concerning the meaning of 1Co 11:15 which says,

> *"But if a woman has long hair, it is a glory to her? For her Hair is given to her as a covering"*

Yes, this verse does speak to the woman's hair as being *her covering*, however I heard the Spirit of the Lord say.....

> *"**until she becomes married!**"*

In other words, when a young woman is unmarried, *"her hair is a symbol of Christ's covering over her."* For an older woman who is unmarried, *"her hair is a symbol of Christ's covering over her.* However, once a woman is married, then the married woman should **COVER** *her* **COVERING** *of hair* on her head, as an out-ward symbol of her *husband's covering authority over her!*

Ephesians 5:23 says,

> *"For the husband is the head of (**authority over**) the wife*
> *as Christ is the head of (**authority over**) the church,"*

The husband is the head of the wife because the woman was created for man..

> *"For man was not made from woman, but woman from man.*
> *Neither was man created for women, but woman for man.*
> *This is why a wife ought to have a symbol of authority on*
> *her head, **because of the angels**." 1 Corinthians 11:8-10*

Now let's dive deeper into understanding the meaning behind the statements, *"a sign/symbol of authority on her head"* and *"because of the angles."*

(a) A Sign and symbol of Authority

Signs ~&~ Symbols

> *"The blood shall be a sign for you, on the houses where*
> *you are. And when I see the blood, I will pass over you,*
> *and no plague will befall you to destroy you, when I*
> *strike the land of Egypt." Exodus 12:13 ESV*

Signs are used to indicate something that is occurring, or going to occur. **Signs** always have a clear meaning, often giving information or an instruction.

Symbols are representations for something, but you need knowledge to understand what the symbol represents. For example, biohazard symbols, restroom and travel symbols, even today's emoji symbols, all need a level of knowledge to understand their meaning.

Another example, in the scriptures, when the blood was put over the doorpost of the Israelite houses, it was a sign of Israel's protective covering from the Lord, which meant the death angel would pass over their homes.

When God sees blood on something that is physical (*like the door posts*) it's a sign and symbol of recognition! To God, blood is a **spiritual symbol** that God recognizes its meaning according to its use. For Israel however, the blood served as a **physical sign** to distinguish the houses they were in, *"so that No plague will fall on you to destroy you when I (the Lord) strike the land of Egypt." Exodus 12:13*

In the same way, angels see **a covering on the head of a woman** according to the *Word of God*, that established man's covering. Therefore, when a woman covers her head in obedience to the word of God, **her head covering is a sign & a symbol** that the angels recognize its meaning according to its use!

This is what I heard in my Spirit,

> *"A woman's head covering is **a symbol** to the angels concerning God's purpose for man; and a woman's head covering is **a sign** to the angels who see according to the word of God."*

So when a woman wears a covering on her head, it's **a symbol to the angels** of the husband's authority over the woman, because woman came FROM man, and the woman was created FOR man, *1 Corinthians 11:8*

AND

When a woman wears a covering on her head it's *a sign to the angels* of Christ's authority, and to carry out the instruction of God by His Word!

Hebrews 1:14 says,

> *Are not all the angels ministering spirits sent out [by God] to serve those who will inherit salvation?*

(b) Because of the Angels?

> *"A woman should wear a symbol of her husband's authority on her head* **because of the Angels,***" 1 Corinthians 11:9-10*

As I read and meditated on this verse over and over again, I heard the Spirit of God tell me to insert the word **"purpose"** so the scripture reads like this,

> *"A woman should wear a symbol of her husband's authority on her head because of the (**purpose of**) Angels"*

Then the Lord said to me,

> *"The Purpose of Angels speaks to the purpose of their creation which is two fold;* **to perform** *the Lord's word &* **to obey** *the voice of the Lord's word,"*

Psalm 103:20 says,

> *"Bless the LORD, you His angels, Mighty in strength, who carry out His word (**His purpose**), Obeying the voice (**the intent**) of His word!"*

We must understand that angels are *"Watchers of the Word."* They *(angels)* are purposed to *perform* and **obey** the authority of God's word! However, according to the scriptures, some of the angels fell from their proper abode because they rebelled against the voice of God's word, *(meaning they disobeyed the intent of His Spirit)* concerning the purpose of man. Instead, these angels followed the intent *(the voice)* of Satan to corrupt the purpose of God through the seed of man,

> *"Now when men began to multiply on the face of the earth and daughters were born to them, the sons of God saw that the daughters of men were beautiful, and they took as wives whomever they chose." Genesis 6:1-2*

> *"The Nephilim were on the earth in those days—and afterward as well—when the sons of God had relations with the daughters of men. And they bore them children who became the mighty men of old, men of renown." Genesis 6:4*

> *"And I remind you of the angels who did not stay within the limits of authority God gave them but left the place where they belonged. God has kept them securely chained in prisons of darkness, waiting for the great day of judgment." Jude 1:6*

Chapter 6

The POWER of AUTHORITY Comes from being UNDER authority!

It's A Spiritual Principle

The Lord said to me,

> "When Lucifer (Satan) was in the presence of God he was a "covering of authority.""

> "A covering means responsible for; Lucifer was a covering Cherub, responsible for covering the intent of God's Glory."

Ezekiel 28:14 says,

> "You were the anointed cherub who covers,"

So where did Satan's authority in heaven come from? Answer, *it came from being under the authority of God's word,*

> *"because the power of authority, comes from being under authority!"*

The Lord said to me,

> *"Satan was under the authority of my Word in heaven, he's under the authority of My Word that you speak on earth!"*

This is not just a statement the Lord said to me, but it's a ***Spiritual principle*** and I'll prove it, through the story of the Roman Centurion.

In the scriptures, the Centurion Roman officer recognizes Jesus as a man of authority because he is a man *under authority,* so the Centurion says,

> *"For I myself (**like you Jesus**) am a man under authority, with soldiers under me"*

Now notice what being under authority empowers the Centurion to do...

He said,

> *"I tell one to go, and he goes; and another to come, and he comes. I tell my servant to do something, and he does it." Matthew 8:9*

The authority that he exercises empowers him to ***instruct and command!*** However, the power of the Roman Centurion doesn't come from himself, but his power comes from the authority he's under! In other words, *the power of authority* he exercises comes from his submission to follow a higher authority's instructions. Therefore his power comes from another source!

What is Authority?

Authority is a power that is from God, it is God's weapon against the enemy. God's authority given to man through Christ is what makes spirits obey us! The authority of the Believer in Christ is the principle by which God rules the earth through man!

Authority is defined as *the creator or originator of a thing. Authority means source.*

Authority is the source from where power comes from! Let me say that again,

> *"Authority is **the source** from where **power** comes from!"*

God is *the source of all power*, which was given to Christ, and Christ submitted to his fathers authority. Jesus said in John 5:30,

> *"I can do nothing on my own authority; I judge only as God tells me, so my judgment is right, because I am not trying to do what I want, **but only what he who sent me wants**." John 5:30 ESV*

And as Christ submits to his fathers authority, he's able to *exercise his fathers authority*, and **then give authority to man...**

> *"And calling His twelve disciples to Him, **Jesus gave them authority** over unclean spirits, so that they could drive them out and heal every disease and sickness."*

*"Heal the sick, raise the dead, cleanse the lepers, drive
out demons. Freely you have received; freely give."*
Matthew 10:1-8

Simply put, through Christ, man has been given legal authorization
(*authority*) to exercise *God's power* over all the Earth!

In Matthew 28:18 Jesus says,

*"All authority in heaven and on earth has been given to
Me. Therefore go and make disciples of all nations, bap-
tizing them in the name of the Father, and of the Son, and
of the Holy Spirit, and teaching them to obey all that I
have commanded you."*

To put it another way Jesus said,

*"All authority in heaven and on earth (**to command and
subdue Spirits**) has been given to Me by my father."
Now Go (**under my authority and in my power**) and
make disciples of all nations by teaching them to obey
(**My authority through**) all that I have commanded you
(**So they can exercise authority**)!*

As Christ's disciples, we obey his authority, so in intern we can
exercise his authority. Why?

*"Because the power of authority, comes from being un-
der authority!"*

All power (like energy) has a source from which it flows. Even
the kingdom of darkness has a hierarchical order from which authority flows. Witches, warlocks, wizards, devils, princes, demons,
thrones, powers, principalities and fallen angels are all subject to
a *hierarchical order of authority*. That means in order to exercise

authority, they have to follow the commands of the hierarchy over them, or they suffer Satan's consequences (which are never good)!

When you try to exercise power without being subject to that power's source of authority, you can bring harm and danger to yourself and others. Do you remember the seven sons of Sceva?

The seven sons of Sceva (a *Jewish High Priest*) tried to use the name of the Lord Jesus **without being under his authority** because they did not believe, and you see what happened to them.

> *Some Jews who traveled around and drove out evil spirits also tried to use the name of the Lord Jesus to do this. They said to the evil spirits, **"I command you in the name of Jesus, whom Paul preaches."** 14 Seven brothers, who were the sons of a Jewish High Priest named Sceva, were doing this.15 But the evil spirit said to them, **"I know Jesus, and I know about Paul; but you—who are you?"** 16 The man who had the evil spirit in him attacked them with such violence that he overpowered them all. They ran away from his house, wounded and with their clothes torn off. Acts 19:13-16*

Simply put, the evil spirit said to them,

> *"I know **Jesus's authority** comes from God, and I know **Paul's authority** comes from Christ, but you, who are you? **Whose authority are you under?**"*

Paul Was Under Authority!

When it comes to the practice of women in the Church covering their head, many people use the argument *"well Paul didn't say it was a command or an instruction from the Lord, therefore women don't have to cover their heads when they pray or prophesy."* But that's not a true statement. The Lord showed me Paul's speaking to the Church of Corinth was a command from the Lord, without him saying *"this is a command from the Lord."* But in order to see what Paul spoke as a command, let's start by understanding what a command is!

A Command is an authoritative direction or instruction to do something.

An **authoritative direction** is given by someone **who has authority!** Paul, an Apostle of Christ was given authority to go and speak to the Gentiles and give them instructions to follow the ways of Christ and His Kingdom...

"Paul, a servant of Christ Jesus, called to be an apostle, and set apart for the gospel of God" Romans 1:1

But the Lord said to him, "Go, for he is a chosen vessel of Mine to bear My name before Gentiles, kings, and the children of Israel." Acts 9:15

Clearly, there were times within the New Testament scriptures when Paul said, ***"This is a command from the Lord,"*** *or when he said* ***"I, not the Lord."*** This means there was a purpose according to the Spirit of God that led Paul to make these distinctive statements at certain points within the text. I call them distinctive statements because as the Spirit of God inspired Paul to write, Paul makes these statements at **precise places within his Epistles.** Nevertheless, whether you believe Paul's instruction that *"a woman should cover her head"* was a command from God or not, it does not negate this truth, that Paul was able to demonstrate in word and in deed the power of Christ's authority, because he was a man under *authority!*

Chapter 7

The Women's Authority in Christ is Restored through her Head!

There are women within the Church who believe they have authority simply because they are *"in Christ,"* so they may think,

"I am in Christ, therefore I don't have to cover my head"

Yes as Believers, we are in Christ, however, God has established *a way* to access Christ's authority. For example, there is a way to receive life, and that's through death! *(meaning we must die to the flesh, and be born again of God's Spirit in order to have life in the Spirit)*

Ladies, I cannot stress this point enough, there is an **order to God's Kingdom!** The realm of God is a realm of order! It is a legalistic realm where God expects all of His creation to conform to His laws and His ways!

In 1 Corinthians 11, Paul reveals by way of instruction to the Church of Corinth, God's *order of authority* which is *man's covering,*

> *"God is the head of Christ,*
> *Christ is the head of man,*
> *Man is the Head of the women.."*
> *1 Corinthians 11*

In the Garden, God told the woman how the consequence of sin, produced within the woman, a desire for her husband's authority *(to instruct her husband)*, but according to God's order, the husband will rule over the woman by authority *(to instruct her)*!

God said,

> *"To the woman, I will greatly multiply Your pain in childbirth, In pain you shall deliver children; Your desire will be for your husband(s' **authority**), Yet he will rule over you (**by authority**)"*

The consequence that God spoke to the woman in Genesis 3, is **the law** that Paul references when he is speaking to the Church of Corinth about God's order,

Paul says,

> *"For God is not a God of disorder, but of peace—as in all the churches of the saints. Women are to be silent in the churches. They are not permitted to speak, but must be in submission, **as the law says**" 1 Corinthians 14:34*

But what law is Paul referring to? He's referring to *the law of sin!*

When God said,

> *"To the woman,"I will greatly multiply Your pain in childbirth, In pain you shall deliver children; Yet your desire will be for your husband, And he shall rule over you." Genesis 3:16 NASB*

God was speaking to the woman (*& the man*) according to *the consequence of sin* that had now become *a law* that would govern the soul and the body. Paul is making reference to the *law of sin* that now governs the women's desire to have authority OVER her husband and to instruct him!

> *To instruct means to give explicit directions or orders to follow.*

That's the desire the *consequence of sin* caused the woman to birth in the earth. We can see the results of this law **governing those women who yield to it today!** From the corporate world, to the White House, to inside the home, women desire to exercise authority over men by way of giving them instruction!

But through a dream the Lord gave me on 1/18/24, The Lord corrected my thinking and renewed my thoughts concerning an instruction I gave my husband; He said to me,

> *"The Spirit feeds the Soul, the Soul doesn't feed the Spirit!"*

Men represent *the spirit of man,* women represent *the soul of man.* Therefore if we are to be fed by our husbands spirit, the woman's role is to *submit* to her husband's authority. SUB in the word **submit** means *under,* "*Wives come under your husband's authority,*" because coming under his authority reinstates your authority!

Let me say that again,

> "*Coming under your husband's authority* **reinstates YOUR** *authority because the woman's authority in Christ is reinstated through submission to her head!*"

Therefore, according to God's *order of authority*, the woman is not submitted to Christ directly, but *the woman submits to Christ through submission to her husband!*

That's why the scripture says,

> "*Wives, submit to your own husbands, as to the Lord.*"
> *Ephesians 5:22*

Did you notice this scripture does not say, "Wives, submit to the Lord?"

> *It says, "Wives, submit to your own husbands, as to the Lord."*

Verse 23 goes on to say,

> "*For* *the husband is the head of the wife* *as Christ is the head of the church, His body, of which He is the Savior. Now as the church submits to Christ, so also wives should submit to their husbands in everything.*"
> *Ephesians 5:23-24*

Now after reading that verse I can hear some of you saying,

"but I am submitted to my husband"

But I hear the Lord God saying,

"You are submitted to your husband, when you wear a symbol of his authority on your head!"

The reality is that you're not submitted under your husband's authority just because you say you are.

I heard the Lord say,

"What you say, is what you demonstrate, because it's what you believe!"

Jesus already proved that we can say or speak words that sound good concerning our faith and our standing in Christ, but those words may not be coming out of a heart that is surrendered to God....

Jesus said "These people honor me with their lips, but their hearts are far from me." Matthew 15:8 NLT

So it's not enough just for us as women to say **"I'm submitted to my husband,"** but there has to be a physical demonstration of the spiritual meaning behind the words we speak.

*"Because on the Earth, words represent **spiritual seeds that bear physical fruit!**"*

For example, it wasn't enough just for God to say *"he loved the world,"* but God, who is Spirit, **demonstrated his unseen love for us through the physical body of Jesus,** his only begotten son.

The Spirit or the seed of God's word came into the earth and was sown in the womb of a woman (*Mary*) who gave birth to Jesus the Christ, who had an earthly physical body, but was the spiritual symbol of God's redeeming love for mankind. So the Word of God that exists in the unseen realm, produced in the natural realm the physical body of Jesus that could be seen.

Even as I'm writing this, the Lord is showing me that there are levels of submission. So I'm not saying that unless you cover your head, you've never submitted to your husband. I am NOT SAYING THAT! But there are women, who may even be reading this book, who do not know about Paul's instructions that a wife should cover her head when she prays or prophecies, *but God sees their heart is in submission to their husbands according to their level of spiritual understanding.* Yes, most of us as wives at times, have been submissive to our husbands instructions, according to the level of our personal relationship with God. So the more we grow in our relationship with Christ, the more our capacity to receive truth like *"head covering"* grows, which means the Spirit of God can reveal *higher levels of understanding in Him.* Given that we can only know and grow in spiritual truth when it is revealed to us.

Now I need you to understand that coming under your husband's authority doesn't just happen automatically when you get married; *NO! You have to place yourself there!*

For example..

You're not fasting simply because you say, "I'm fasting." No! You fast when you choose to submit your soul to God; and that inward submission of your soul (*your heart*) to God shows outwardly, *through the action of abstaining from eating food.* Fasting from eating food, is an outward symbol for the humbling that's taking place on the inside of your soul.

Let me say it like this, being submitted to your husband's authority, isn't just about you following your husband's instructions just for the sake of following his instructions (*because he says so*). No! You're placing yourself under the authority *"that he speaks,"* so that angels who carry out the word of God, **"respond to the Word of God that you speak!"**

Therefore as married women, if we want to activate our authority in Christ, we must walk in obedience to *God's order of authority*, and honor our head (*husband*) by wearing a sign of his authority on our head.

DIShonor is a form of DISobedience!

> *"And every woman who prays or prophesies with her head uncovered **dishonors her head**," 1Co 11:5*

So what does it mean to *dishonor* your head/husband? I thought it only meant to disrespect my husband, which is true, but the Lord expounded. He showed me that when I dishonor my husband (*my head*), I'm also in *disobedience to God my father*, because **"Dishonor** is a form of **Disobedience**," and "**Honor** is a form of **Obedience**."

Dishonor=Disobedience
Honor=Obedience

Ephesians 6:1-3 says,

> *"Children, **obey** your parents in the Lord, for this is right"*

In this verse the writer is telling *"children to obey their parents."* However, when children become an adult, the writer changes the language from *obey* to *honor* and says,

> *"Honor your father and mother this is the first commandment with a promise, that it may go well with you and that you may live long in the land." Ephesians 6:1-3*

To be clear, children **Obey** but adults **Honor!** Let me say that again, *children **obey**, and adults **honor!***

> *"I heard in my Spirit, "Submitting brings honor."*

As an adult, I honor my husband, and as a child of God I obey my father's instructions! Since everything first starts in the unseen realm, then manifests into the physical realm, my *obedience to my heavenly father's word is first,* which leads me to submit and honor my husband;

let me say that again,

> *"My obedience to my heavenly father, **leads me to submit, and Honor my husband!**"*

And it's my ***disobedience*** to my heavenly fathers word, that will lead me to ***dishonor*** my husband who is my head!

This is what I heard the Spirit of God saying,

> *"You're not walking in authority when you're walking **in dishonor** which is another form of **disobedience!** Dishonor is disobedience which **is sin.**"*

The Lord showed me that when we're in disobedience (*whether we know it or not*) we are in sin, because disobedience doesn't involve our knowledge of sin, it involves our willingness to comply with it! It's our compliance with sin that brings disobedience!

However..,

When you know, meaning your knowledge is involved in your choice to sin, it's no longer ignorance but rebellion! For example, Eve knew what God commanded the man, so she rebelled against the word of God that said,

> "*You must not eat from the tree of the knowledge of good and evil; for in the day that you eat of it, you will surely die.*" *Genesis 2:16 BSB*

And the man Adam as a son, was disobedient to God his father because he *COMPLIED* with what the woman said!

> And to Adam he said, "**Because you have listened to the voice of your wife** and have eaten of the tree of **which I commanded you, 'You shall not eat of it,'** cursed is the ground because of you;"

The man complied with the voice of the woman. He didn't ask Eve any questions, he just took the fruit she gave him and ate it!

The Lord showed me this is what I had done with *the knowledge of women covering their heads.* I had stuck my head down in the sand, I didn't ask any questions, I didn't seek God for understanding, I just complied with **the voice of the world** and **the voice of my flesh**; and may I say I complied very well!

Sure I was aware of women within the body of Christ who practiced covering their heads, but I thought it was mainly the Amish, or women who were extremely radical about their faith. On the other hand, I also knew that Paul spoke about women *covering their heads* in the scriptures. Nevertheless, instead of me seeking God for understanding concerning why Paul was speaking to the Church of Corinth about women covering their heads, I chose to yield to the world's view & the Church's shouts of

"Head covering is not for today, it was according to the culture of that time."

Thus I was okay remaining ignorant to my heavenly fathers ways, dishonoring my husband *(even though at the time I didn't see it that way)*, all the while thinking I was exercising spiritual authority.

The full strength of who we are in Christ, can not be developed in righteousness when we comply with ignorance or disobedience.

Ephesians 4:18 tells us about the effects of ignorance,

> *"So I tell you this, and insist on it in the Lord, that you must no longer walk as the Gentiles do, in the futility of their thinking. They are darkened in their understanding and alienated from the life of God because of the ignorance that is in them **due to the hardness of their hearts.***"*
> *Ephesians 4:18*

Did you hear that? Having a hard heart causes ignorance which alienates us from the life of God, which means ignorance can keep us from being everything God intended for us to be in Him! Now please understand what I am saying, of course we don't know everything, but what we do know, is according to what God has revealed.

Hosea 4:6 says, "My people are destroyed for lack of knowledge;"

The New Living Translation says it this way,

> "My people are being destroyed **because they don't know me.**"

To paraphrase, *"they don't know My Ways,"* because to know God is to know His ways.

There is a knowledge of God that is being revealed, even now, through the writings and reading of this book. God is revealing to the reader, the knowledge of His divine will, for His children to come under *the covering of Christ through submission to God's order of authority,* so we can exercise His authority over the earth!

Chapter 8

COVERING From The Perspective of The Spirit

The Lord showed me that *"Covering is a Power,"* it is an *"authority"* in the realm of the spirit. There are *different types of coverings* in the spiritual realms of God. For example, *authority is a type of covering* in the spirit, and the authority of God's Word (*which is the highest*) is the *covering over man's spirit*, which functions differently from the grace of God that is a *covering over man's soul*.

The Lord said to me *"ignorance is also a type of covering."* It's a covering of darkness that is purposed to hide and veil the knowing of Truth. This is why God's will is not for us to choose to be ignorant of spiritual things, because it's choosing to be under a *spiritual covering of* darkness that God has NOT called man into, but God has called us out of darkness and into His marvelous light! 1 Peter 2:9

I Heard, "Every Spirit Has A Covering!"

As the Lord began to give me more understanding of *"covering,"* He started showing me what **Covering IS** *(meaning how it works)*, through my experience with Black culture and their obsession with Greek sororities and fraternities.

This is what I heard the Spirit of the Lord saying to those who are under the Spirit of a Greek letter organization,

He said,

> *"The Letters on your chest represent a **Spiritual Covering** over your Soul. A spiritual covering has a certain level of authority over you. The spiritual covering comes from **a spiritual altar that was raised** and dedicated to a spiritual deity (Greek God or Goddess); but who is the spiritual covering of authority over a fraternity or sorority's Greek God? For every spirit has **a covering!** It's either a covering of **darkness or light!**"*

Coverings function in a *hierarchical order of authority*, according to their purpose. Therefore do not be fooled! All spirits, (even spirits who lead men to create mythological Greek gods) have a higher *covering source of authority* that they submit and answer to!

So the question I heard the Lord ask those who belong to a Greek Letter organization is,

> *"Who is the higher covering **source of authority** over your sororities and fraternities Greek God? Who do the Greek Gods and goddesses of the divine 9 submit to? **Yahweh** or **Satan?**"*

Many of us within the church have been deceived to believe that we can blend and mix with the things of the world on neutral ground. However there is no neutral middle ground that is pleasing or acceptable to the Lord! Therefore it is crucial that we understand that *coverings of darkness* and *coverings of light* cannot dwell together! Consequently we must choose! Choose to live under the *covering of light only!*

This led me to ask the Lord a question..

"How do you know when you're under a covering?"

The Lord said, "What You Submit to, Covers You!"

Whether it's the covering of a church, a husband, a religion, philosophy or ideology, a government system, sorority, fraternity, or the culture of the world; whatever you're submitted to in your heart, covers you!

It was after this revelation that I realized, this book is dealing with **Spiritual Covering!** This book is not just about *a woman's submission* to her husband shown by wearing a physical garment over her head, but this book uncovers the truth,

"What you submit to, COVERS you!"

This truth applies to men and women! **Submission to authority produces covering!** The submission of man's soul (*heart*) to Christ's authority, is submission to Christ as man's covering! This is when I heard the Lord tell me to change the name of this book, from

"The power of Submission" to *"The Power of Covering!"*

I Heard, "A Covering Is A Protection"

"And the man and his wife were both naked and were not ashamed." **Genesis 2:25**

The man and his wife were naked and unashamed in the Garden because the Spirit of man was **covered by the word of God,** which *protected* and *prevented* the man and the woman from seeing themselves apart from how God saw them!

The Lord said to me,

*"A covering **protects** how we see,"*

In other words one of the purposes for *a covering* is to ensure how we see, agrees with **how our covering sees!** There are two kingdoms fighting to protect, and to control how man sees.

This is what I mean; God and His kingdom are fighting to keep man **covered and seeing** according to the light of Christ, but Satan and his kingdom are fighting against God's intentions. Satan's kingdom presents to man a perverted **covering and way of seeing through the world that is evil but masked as good.** *Satan's covering* through the world's systems is not a protection that is good for man's soul. Satan's purpose for covering is intended to mask and conceal, to restrict man's access to truth, so man continues to see through the source of darkness, instead of man seeing through the source of light which is Christ!

As this was being revealed to me, I began to understand why it's so important to be married to a Godly man who walks with Christ as his covering & his source! For if the husband's covering is Christ, then *the husband's covering authority* over the wife is purposed to protect her spiritual sight grounded in Christ! Due to how the husband sees *(which is according to his covering)* will be how the wife sees also! This process of thought led to the next statement I heard the Spirit of God saying....

"The Covering DETERMINES How We See!"

As long as the man & the woman remained in the Garden, they were covered by the word of God, which means they saw themselves according to the word! However, as soon as they rejected God's covering and took on another covering *(of flesh)*, *they saw themselves according to that COVERING, which was according to the darkness of the flesh!*

> *"And the eyes of both of them were opened, and they knew that they were naked;* ***so they sewed together fig leaves and made coverings for themselves."*** *Genesis 3:7*

Adam and Eve saw themselves as flesh according ***to their covering*** *(which was the mind of the flesh controlled by Satan.)* Satan not only gave the man & the woman access to knowledge that God did not intend, but this knowledge gave them the understanding they were physically naked. Consequently, they could see the physical nakedness of their body, with their physical eyes, but they could no longer see the spiritual nakedness of their soul! That's because they could no longer see themselves spiritually through the eyes of man's spirit, which meant they could no longer understand the things of God's Spirit!

I begin to see the effects of this through an unbelieving husband who's *covering* is not Christ, but the flesh.

Consequently, even when a *husband's covering is of the flesh*, God has still purposed the husband to teach, feed, correct and lead his wife and family according to how *his covering sees*. This is why it's important **not** to be unequally yoked in marriage. If the wife believes in Christ, but the husband does not, then when the husband tries to lead, feed, teach or correct his wife *(according to his covering)*, it can and will cause quarrels, arguments, and chaos within the home, which impacts a woman to be non submissive to her husband.

Jesus said, "Take My yoke upon you and learn from me"
Matthew 11:29 ESV

When we take on someone's yoke we take on their spirit, which acts as *a covering*. That spirit or *covering*, teaches us how to see according to it. Have you ever noticed when a man or woman is under a person's teaching, they begin to sound and act just like that person? That's because their mannerisms, the way they speak or behave resemble the ***Spirit of the covering*** their under.

For example, God *(who is Spirit)* is the source of Christ, and what Christ sees his father *(his covering)* do, that's what he does, and what Christ hears his father *(his covering)* say, that's what he says.

John 12:49-50 says,

> *"I don't speak on my own authority. The Father who sent me has commanded me what to say and how to say it. And I know his commands lead to eternal life; so I say whatever the Father tells me to say."*

> *"Truly, truly, I say to you, the Son can do nothing of his own accord, but only what he sees the Father doing. For whatever the Father does, that the Son does likewise.*
> *John 5:19*

My sister-in-law told me one time after reading *a word from the Lord* that I posted on one of my social media platforms, that I spiritually sound so much like my husband, that she forgot she was reading a post I wrote, and she assumed she was reading one of his posts!

All Coverings Have A Purpose!

Whether it's a physical covering like a house, or the spiritual covering of a relationship, *all coverings function according to purpose!* Things like government systems are a *covering*, the family unit and the husband are *coverings,* your job is a *covering*, social and fraternal organizations are a *covering,* cultural organizations *are a covering,* clothes over the body and hair wigs are *all coverings* that function according to purpose.

Whatever covering you're under in this physical realm, is because parallelled in the spirit realm, you're under a covering! The *covering in the spirit realm* has a purpose, which influences your seeing according to a source. That source is either a source of light or darkness, Christ or Satan! The problem is we don't realize the people, systems, and organizations we are under, *function as coverings,* that either enable or hinder our ability to see the truth.

That's why it's important to understand that God's order of authority *is a covering that protects our soul* from falling prey and to *another covering's purpose* that is not from God! Therefore, we should learn to trust and depend on the Holy Spirit's help, to reconnect and align our spiritual seeing and understanding to the perspective of Christ, so we see God's intent *for His covering* correctly, according to the perspective of His Spirit!

Chapter 9

COVERING From the perspective of the Garden

I Believe that most people today view the practice of
"head covering" *physically from the perspective of the flesh. So I want to share a spiritual picture the Lord showed me concerning* ***"covering"*** *from the beginning, from the spiritual perspective of the Garden.*

1 Corinthians 11:5-6 says,

"And every woman who prays or prophesies with her head uncovered dishonors her head, for it is just as if her head were shaved. If a woman does not cover her head, she should have her hair cut off. And if it is shameful for a woman to have her hair cut or shaved off, ***she should cover her head."***

Paul said,

> *"And Every woman who prays or prophesies, she should cover her head."*

But why is Paul saying this? Where is he getting this idea from? In order to answer this question we must go back to the beginning, from within the Garden. However let's first start with understanding what it means to *prophesy*.

> *Prophecy - is the inspired declaration of God's divine will and purpose.*

> To **Prophesy,** *is to Foretell & to Forthtell the mind of God, and the divine will of God.*

Anytime we speak God's will concerning a word He has spoken directly to us or spoken through the scriptures, you're bringing forth and declaring *the will of God.* This is what the woman in the garden did, she spoke the divine will of God to the serpent...

> *"The woman answered the serpent, "We may eat the fruit of the trees of the garden, but about the fruit of the tree in the middle of the garden, **God has said, 'You must not eat of it or touch it, or you will die."*** *Genesis 3:2 NASB*

The woman made a prophetic declaration to the serpent, forthtelling God's divine will for man! What was God's will? That man must **not eat from the tree of the knowledge of good and evil...**

> *And the LORD God commanded him, "You may eat freely from every tree of the garden, but you must not eat from the tree of the knowledge of good and evil" Genesis 2:17 BSB*

So the woman not only prophesied God's will to the serpent, but she made a prophetic declaration making known the consequence and the condition that would occur, which was death!

> *"God has said, 'You must not eat of it or touch it, **or you will die.**" Genesis 3:2 BSB*

> *NOTE:[Even with her added statement **"or touch it"** the prophetic consequence she declared was still the same, death!]*

And here's the spiritual picture I hope you see by the Spirit of God, that as the woman prophesied God's will to the serpent, you guessed it, **the head of the woman was covered!** Her head was covered *spiritually* because she was under the authority of God's word through her husband!

> *"As the woman in the garden spoke the command of God to the serpent, her **head** (her husband) was **covered** by the word of God."*

Wait, the man was covered? Doesn't the scripture say that *"the man and his wife were both naked,"* meaning they were without a covering? Well, naked can mean that, however this is what I was shown: The garden of Eden represented *a consciousness,* a place that provided what I heard the Lord call an *"intermediate covering"* over the spirit of man, by the word of God.

Naked and Not Ashamed

> *"And the man and his wife were both naked (without understanding of evil) and were **not ashamed** (without guilt).*

In this scripture, **naked** and **not ashamed** are not literal references of man seeing his physical naked body, but they are references to the spiritual condition of man's spirit and soul, which had **not** been exposed to evil. In the garden, man's spirit and soul were exposed *only to the knowledge of God*, which is good!

Therefore *"they were naked,"* is not a reference to the covering they didn't have, on the contrary, it's a reference to the covering they did have! The man was *covered by the word of God!*

This is what I heard,

> *"While in the garden, the command 'You must not eat from the tree of the knowledge of good and evil,' was an intermediate Covering."*

> *Intermediate - means being or occurring at the middle place, or stage.*

In other words, the garden of Eden represented *a womb*, a middle place of consciousness where man's choice would be birthed; and through the command, *the word of God* provided a *"middle place Covering"* over man that was temporary, until man's **choice** was birthed!

This is what I heard,

> *"They (the man and the woman) had not chosen God (by partaking from the tree of life) to be their permanent covering." (A covering that would last or remain unchanged indefinitely.)*

It was in this middle place of consciousness that contained the **CHOICE,** between the consciousness of l*ife (God's permanent covering) and the consciousness of death.*

> *"And in the middle of the garden were the tree of life and the tree of the knowledge of good and evil."*
> Genesis 2:9 BSB

Put simply, the man chose to listen to the voice of his wife, and the woman was deceived. They both became subject to the *covering authority* of another consciousness, which was *a lesser covering* and a perverted way of seeing through the eyes of the flesh!

> *"And **the eyes of both of them were opened,** and they knew that they were naked;"*Genesis 3:7

This is what I heard,

> *"The knowledge of good and evil **is a Covering!** It's a way of seeing that is through knowledge, that produces insufficiency."*

Satan became the man and the woman's ***spiritual Covering through knowledge,*** which led man to create an alternate world and reality through the ***mind of the flesh*** which controls how man's soul sees in the earth.

Therefore ladies, submission to our head (*our husbands/our covering*) protects us. It's a spiritual defense against deception!

Chapter 10

There's a Difference Between Anointing ~&~ Authority

In my Spirit I heard,

> "There's a difference between **anointing** and **authority**. Both flow from the same source (from God), but they function and operate differently according to purpose."

So What is Anointing?

Anointing is the empowerment (*by God's Spirit*) to accomplish a specific purpose in God. When someone or something is anointed, it means God has chosen who or what He will work through to bring about His purpose. For example, the prophet Isaiah said,

"The Spirit of the Lord is upon me, (why?) because he has anointed me (chosen to work through me, for a specific purpose) to proclaim good news to the poor."
Isaiah 61:1

2 Chronicles 22:7 says,

"When Ahaziah arrived, he went out with Joram to meet Jehu son of Nimshi, whom the LORD had anointed to destroy the house of Ahab."

To put it another way, an *anointing* is a vehicle or instrument that God's power flows through to fulfill His assigned purpose. **Anointing** speaks more to **"the operation of God"** meaning **"how"** God brings forth his purpose, not just to the power of God.

Acts 10:38 speaks to anointing as *"how"* God brings forth his purpose. Verse 38 says,

*"You know of Jesus of Nazareth, **how God anointed** (operated through) Him **with the Holy Spirit and with power,** and how He went about doing good and healing all who were oppressed by the devil, for God was with Him."*

Many believers within the church have conflated the term *anointing and authority*, to mean the same thing...*power!* (*I thought that too*). However the Lord showed me there are many people *including prominent charismatic women of faith who do NOT cover their heads,* who operate in His anointing, but do not exercise His power of authority!

Anointing does not mean power, it means *to empower*..

Anointing is the *empowerment* by God's Spirit to accomplish a specific purpose. Even though most people use the word *empowerment* and *power* interchangeably, they have different meanings.

Empower(ment) means to equip with the necessary tools and resources to accomplish a specific objective or purpose. The tools and resources that God uses to empower someone are abundant; from wisdom, knowledge, & understanding to teaching, speaking and preaching, along with skill sets and crafts of every kind just to name a few. These are "how" God brings forth his purposes.

Power on the other hand, is the ability to influence or control by dominance and authority. Power is the capacity to make things happen to achieve a desired outcome.

Yes, both *anointing & authority* come from God, because He is the source; but **how** they operate is what makes the difference, because *the power of authority* is given to those who are under authority!

*Authority is a power that **is given** to a person who has yielded or surrendered their will to another. Therefore you can never TAKE authority, it has to be given. Contrary to popular belief within the Church, you don't take authority just because you say, "**I'm taking authority.**" You cannot GIVE authority that you are NOT under!*

The truth is, any man or woman of God who does not submit themselves under authority *cannot exercise the power of authority!*

They may, however, exercise an expression of God through *an anointing!*

For example, there are many well known women within the Church (*who do not cover their head*) that preach, pray and prophesy the word of God over large congregations and social media platforms, who are **anointed by God** to fulfill a specific purpose in God. Yet they do not exercise **authoritative power,** and that's because one cannot exercise the *authority of God*, and be in *disobedience to the word of God* at the same time. Unfortunately, this is the case within the Church body. Many are **in disobedience** when it comes to following Paul's instructions that a woman should *"cover her head when she prays or prophesies." 1 Corinthians 11:3-16*

However, when it comes to having an **anointing,** because of the *grace of God*, we may be in disobedience to God, yet we are still able to exercise God's anointing! How? By reason of God's anointing that doesn't take man's obedience or belief to operate!

There were many kings and prophets in the scriptures who were anointed or used by God, **not** because of their faith in the God of Israel, but because they were chosen by God to fulfill God's purpose (*for example King Cyrus Isaiah 45:3-7 and King Nebuchadnezzar Ezra 5:12*).

> *"God's anointing remained upon them until God's purpose was fulfilled."*

This is what occurred during the reign of King Saul. When God's anointing was removed from King Saul, it was not because of his disobedience, but it was because God's purpose for using him (*to bring David into his service*) was fulfilled.

Romans 11:29 says, *"For the gifts and the calling of God are irrevocable."*

God's anointing operates by the Spirit of God, as well as the grace of God, and is maintained by the will of God! Therefore, *God's anointing* does not function according to obedience or belief, however the power of authority does!

The Power of Authority operates by belief and obedience!

Chapter 11

Your BELIEF Exercises Your AUTHORITY!

Most people within the church (*especially those who lead*) want to exercise power, but they either don't know how to connect to the power, or they don't want to submit to the commands of the source of authority that is behind the power!

Nevertheless, there is **one word** the Lord showed me, connects His people to the power source of Christ...

*That word is **Belief!***

I heard the Spirit of God say,

"When you believe, the power (source) you're connected to, will begin to flow."

Belief in God through Christ is how we manifest the power of Christ's Kingdom on Earth! I further heard the Spirit of God saying,

> *"My Spirit connects you to my power, but your **belief activates my power**, because when you believe, your **belief submits you to authority!**"*

Let me say it this way,

> *When we believe, it's our belief that submits us (to authority) to follow and do what the word says!"*

I've learned this is why I am able to submit to my husband's authority, because *I believe* that his instructions over our family are for our good! *I believe* his instructions will produce a favorable outcome for me and our family.

Let me use another example. Those who are in the branches of our military, have learned to believe and follow the word of instruction coming down from the person of authority they are under. If this wasn't true, our military would be in disorder and chaos! When you don't believe the person of authority over you (like your husband, your boss, or your government) knows what they're talking about, or if you don't believe their intentions over you are good, you will NOT follow their instructions. You will not submit to the authority of their words!

This is what many people experienced around the world, when governments began to mandate their citizens to take the COVID-19 vaccines. Those who did not trust the knowledge behind the science, and did *not believe* their government's intentions were good, did not submit *to their governments authority*. Instead many people protested against the instructions of government lockdowns, and they defied and rejected government mandates to be vaccinated.

Well, this same principle of *"belief"* applies to our faith. When you do not believe the *word of God,* you will not submit and do what the word says! Therefore you cannot exercise Christ's authority, when you do not submit to Christ, who is the source of that power!

When the Spirit of God's word comes to you, to correct, reveal, to instruct or rebuke... by faith only believe! Choose to believe the Spirit of God's word that is revealed through the reading of the scriptures. There is a spirit behind the meaning of all scripture, *"which is given by inspiration of God, and is profitable for doctrine, for reproof, for correction, for instruction in righteousness, so that the man of God may be complete, fully equipped for every good work." 2 Timothy 3:16*

Choose to believe the Rhema word of God that you discern *(by your Spirit)* when it's revealed, because belief is what submits us to authority *(to do the instruction we hear)*, and it takes belief to exercise Christ's power.

This is what the passage about the Roman Centurion demonstrates:

> *"Then Jesus said to the centurion, "Go!* **As you have believed***," Matthew 8:13 BSB*

The Centurion believed the *power of the word of Christ* because he understood the **principle of authority**. Therefore he believed all Jesus had to do was *say the word,* and his servant would be healed!

The function of Authority

The Lord showed me how *the power of His word* functions for us, in the realm of the spirit when we believe. He showed me *the power of the word & the authority of the word.*

The Power of The Word is our (**defense**), it is our ammunition that protects, defends, and defeats the spiritual forces of darkness that come against us.

The Authority of the Word is our (**offense**), it is our weapon that uses the power of the word (the ammunition) to send angels to attack, stop and defeat the spiritual forces of darkness that come against us!

Angels are subject to the word of God, they are not subject to us. So if we are not submitted under the *authority of the word of God,* then we have no power to speak the word of God, that instructs angels. Angels don't respond to our words, angels hearken to the voice of God's command, and they carry out His word! *Psalms 103:20*

Therefore when we believe, we submit to the word, and God sends His angels to respond to **the Word of God we speak; to fight and to defend us!** This is the purpose of angels in the earth, to assist man in bringing the purpose of God, *through the word of God* to pass on earth as it is in heaven!

> *"So My word that proceeds from My mouth will not return to Me empty, but it will accomplish what I please, and it will prosper where I send it." Isaiah 55:11*

These are the weapons of our warfare that are mighty through God, to the pulling down of strongholds! *2 Corinthians 10:4*

The Purpose of Authority

The Lord showed me that growing in the **knowledge of God** involves **knowing what God Wants**. So what does God want?

*"For man to **Subdue** and **Have Dominion** over the Earth!"*

This is the original plan (idea) and purpose of God for man since the beginning of the creation of the heavens and the earth!

*Subdue means - to bring under control; **To bring a territory under control***

*"So God created man in His own image; in the image of God He created him; male and female He created them. Then God blessed them, and God said to them, **"Be fruitful and multiply; fill the earth and subdue it;** have dominion over the fish of the sea, over the birds of the air, and over every living thing that moves on the earth."*
Genesis 1:27-28

In other words the purpose of man being placed on the earth, is so that man could exercise Christ's authority and *"subdue"* the earth. We are purposed to bring the earth under the control of God's Kingdom of light, and have dominion over the fish of *the sea (over the spirits in that realm of the earth)*, over the **birds of the air** *(over the spirits in that realm of the earth)*, and over every living thing that moves on *the earth/the Ground (over the spirits of that realm of the earth)*.

The purpose for our authority is to subdue the earth according to God's Kingdom of light, and then rule by dominion over the things *(the spirits of darkness, principalities, powers, spiritual wickedness in high places)* in those territories, *(your communities, your cities, your towns, country and nations)* through Christ's authority!

This is why it's important for women in Christ to be covered under their husbands' authority, and wear an outward covering *(a symbol of their husbands authority)* on their head. Since it's through **prayer** and **prophecy** that angels are activated to perform God's word to help mankind fulfill God's will on earth as it is in heaven. Therefore in order to subdue, we must speak what God said!

Yet if we're in disobedience and dishonor to our covering of authority *(our husband)*, even though we may be anointed, we're not enabled to exercise Christ's authority. Additionally without Christ's power of authority, we cannot *subdue* and exercise *dominion* for the purpose of establishing God's kingdom.

Therefore I heard the Spirit of God say,

"Don't stop at your Anointing, walk in Christ's authority!"

Chapter 12

We Cover our HEAD, not our Hair!

I want to make the distinction between women of the christian faith, and women of different faiths who also practice covering. We christian women cover our heads according to *the purpose of Christ,* not for the purpose of modesty as in other faiths. In the Christian faith *we cover the head* (*the top/crown, sides, and back*) so if our hair is long, depending on the type of head covering, you may see a woman's hair draped on the shoulders or in a ponytail hanging down her back; and that's okay because *we're covering our head, not our hair!*

So in this last chapter, I want to deal with questions you probably have about head covering, (*I know I had a lot*) from some of the things I've experienced with God on this journey. However, I will say that I'm by far no expert on the subject of *head covering*. The Lord revealed this knowledge to me in 2022, and I'm still growing in my understanding about this subject. The following questions are the questions that I had as God took me through this experience, and the answers are according to my understanding (*so far*) that God revealed.

Here's **question #1,**

> *"Does God expect a woman to cover her head all the time 24 hours a day?*

The answer I heard, **NO!**

Then the Lord asked me a question, he said,

> *"What Spiritual thing (concerning my faith) do I do 24 hours a day non stop?"*

My answer: **NOTHING**

It was at that moment the Lord changed my perspective **to focus on purpose**! I learned that women of Islamic faith do not wear a covering on their head 24 hours a day non stop. A woman of Islamic faith may remove her head covering or Hijab for personal comfort while in the presence of immediate family members; but when a woman is in the presence of people of the opposite sex that are NOT close family members, that's when they wear their Hijab. In other words Muslim women **cover according to purpose!**

God said to me,

> *"The purpose of a head covering is exercised when you pray or prophesy"*

There is a **PURPOSE** why we cover! As believing women in Christ, we are not just aimlessly covering our head all day and night without understanding. The purpose for covering our head is not to please men, the purpose is not to fulfill a religious requirement, for a cultural look, or for the purpose of modesty. The purpose for a Christian woman covering her head, *is to exercise Christ's spiritual authority over the earth* when she prays or prophesies! We cover our heads to fulfill God's purpose through Christ in man on earth!

This brings me to the next question

Question #2

> "Does God expect a woman to cover her head **everytime** she prays?

The answer I heard,

> "God expects a woman to cover her head according to the nature of her prayer."

In other words, the **type of prayer** you're praying determines the need for a head covering. What are you praying about? There are many different types of prayers. Are you praying a *prayer of intercession, prayers of warfare, prayers of agreement or prophetic prayers?* Any speech that requires the exercising of authority *(saying what God said)* requires a woman to cover her head.

However, when we are praying and communing intimately with God our father in His presence, *(giving thanks, praising, worshiping God, and hearing from God)*, this is when I don't need to wear a covering on my head. The Lord showed me if I'm not exercising authority, just speaking intimately with my heavenly father, I do not need to cover. Remember, a *woman's head covering is an outward symbol of authority for spirits to see*, like Satan, angels, demons & devils, principalities, powers, thrones, and spiritual wickedness in high places. Therefore if you're not waring in the realm of the spirit, against spirits, then a physical head covering is not required.

However, from day to day, we don't always know when we're going to need to engage in spiritual warfare through *prophecy or prayer*. This is why I choose to stay ready by wearing a scarf around my neck *when I'm outside of my house in public spaces*. I want to be ready to cover my head, and give full expression to Christ's authority *(by saying what God said)* through prayer and by the laying on of hands at any given moment!

Ephesians 6:18 says,

> *"Pray in the Spirit at all times, with every kind of prayer and petition. To this end, stay alert with all perseverance in your prayers for all the saints."*

1 Thessalonians 5:17 says,

> *"Pray without ceasing."*

That moment could be while I'm driving in my car, when I'm in the store, when I'm at my kids school, when I'm at the movies, out to eat, visiting friends and family, or in the grocery store line. Whenever and wherever I am, I want to be ready and available for the power of God's kingdom to make an impact in someone's life! However, I have experienced by trial and error, times that I thought *I was available* for God's power to move through me, but in reality *I wasn't ready* because I wasn't honoring my husband by covering my head.

*"Through this journey of **head covering**, I noticed a change in the purpose for why I was covering my head. At first, my head covering was all the time out of the fear of the Lord, meaning I didn't want to be in disobedience to my father (which is a good thing not a bad thing). However, now I see another reason, or purpose, why I have become **intentional** about covering my head; and it's because when you begin to walk in the authority of Christ, His Spirit gives you the desire to seek to exercise His authority everywhere you go!"*

How should I Cover?

How you cover depends on your style! You can use scarves, baseball hats, knit hats, fedora hats, wide brim felt hats, straw hats, you name it, it's up to you. But I will be honest with you. According to my experience, finding just the right hat or colored scarf or even how to wear the scarf on your head, might be challenging at first when you're not used to wearing a *"covered head look."* I equate head covering to wearing my hair in its natural state, because it may take time to find what works for you so that you feel confident and pretty. For me, I like to wear colorful or bedazzled scarves that I wear around my shoulders, ready to use as a covering when I'm having date night with my husband, or I'm at a wedding, or any function where I want to wear my hair down, but also be ready in case I need to cover my head.

I also discovered that sometimes when I decide to wear a headscarf, to keep from looking like I'm *"ready for bed,"* I have to put on a little more makeup than usual, and maybe spruce up my outfit, just to make myself feel pretty. Like everything concerning our faith, there is a sacrifice that you make, so you will have to "count the cost," *to cover or not to cover,* that is the question!

The Power of God is a Result of the Presence of God!

If you are a woman of God within the church who "thinks" you are under your husband's authority, God doesn't want you to think, He wants you to KNOW! However this kind of *knowing* doesn't come from studying the scriptures by intellect alone. This *knowing* doesn't come from reading my experience in this book alone; this is a *knowing of truth* that has to be revealed by the *presence of God* through intimacy with God, with our spirit, *through submission of the soul!*

The presence of God creates an experience for *you to know who God is.* In other words the presence of God is the experience of God, and the power of God! One of the things that the presence of God produces....is power!

I heard the Spirit of God say,

> *"The power of God is carried by those who are **submitted** and **surrendered** to Christ's authority!*

Okay, but what's the difference between *submission and surrender?*

- *Submission* is the choice the soul makes; the choice is the action of the soul surrendering to the will of God...
- *Surrender* is the **REST!** The submission of the soul leads to rest! Those who have surrendered *to* God, are at rest *in* God!

Hebrews 4:10 says

> *"For the one who has entered His rest has himself also rested from his works, as God did from His."*

In closing, when we are **submitted** and **surrendered** to the spirit of God, then the presence of God can work, while we *(through the soul)* rest; because the **presence of God**, brings *"the Rest"* of God!

So, are you ready to enter his rest and experience,

The Power of "HIS Covering!"

"Therefore let's make every effort to enter that rest, so that no one will fall by following the same example of disobedience."

"Today if you hear His voice,
Do not harden your hearts."
Hebrews 3:15

ACKNOWLEDGEMENT

I would like to first thank *my Lord and Savior Jesus Christ* for using me, training me and equipping me through the revealed knowledge of this book, to be a voice of truth for His people in these last days. To you God be all glory!

> *"If any man speaks, let him speak as the oracles of God;*
> *if any man minister, let him do it as of the ability which*
> *God giveth: that God in all things may be glorified*
> *through Jesus Christ to whom be praise and dominion*
> *for ever and ever." 1 Peter 4:11*

I would also like to thank my husband Eugene Jackson *"my bae,"* *"my best friend," and "my covering"* for the spiritual oversight of this book. Thank you for your words of wisdom, correction, encouragement, your love, your motivation, and patience with me throughout this endeavor. I love you, and I could not have done this without YOU!

I also want to thank my children David and Amari, for your patience with me, and for giving me the space and the quiet time I needed to get my writing done early in the mornings.

To my bestie Tiffany Payne, I love you! Thank you so much for taking on the task of proofreading and editing this book. Thank you for supporting me throughout this whole spiritual journey, for your words of encouragement and for your direction that helped me get this book published! You are truly the bestie for life! Thank You!

I also would like to thank my sister in Christ Courtney McClain for your prayers, and for being my spiritual springboard and the spiritual ear that I needed, as I worked to sort through and understand *"the knowledge of covering"* the Lord was revealing to me for this book.

And last but certainly not least I would like to thank YOU the reader for buying this book. Your choice to buy this book *as a tool to aid you in your spiritual growth* with Christ, is invaluable, appreciated and a blessing to me, and from the bottom of my heart I say..

THANK YOU!